*Leader's Guide
for group study of*

Meet Yourself in the Psalms

WARREN W. WIERSBE

Leader's Guide prepared by
EMILY NICHOLSON

Twelve Multiuse Transparency Masters (for visual aids) are included in a removable center section. Instructions for using the Multiuse Transparency Masters are on pages 5-6.

VICTOR

BOOKS a division of SP Publications, Inc.
WHEATON, ILLINOIS 60187

Offices also in
Whitby, Ontario, Canada
Amersham-on-the-Hill, Bucks, England

ISBN: 0-88207-895-X

General Preparation

Survey the entire *Text* and this *Leader's Guide*. *This is basic.* Underline important passages in the text and make notes as ideas come to you, before you forget them. Become familiar with the entire course, including all units in the *Guide* that you will be using in your study. A general knowledge of what is coming up later will enable you to conduct each session more effectively and to keep discussion relevant to the subject at hand. If questions are asked that will be considered later in the course, postpone discussion until that time.

Add to your teaching notes any material and ideas you think important or of special help to your class. As teacher, your enthusiasm for the subject and your personal interest in those you teach, will in large measure determine the interest and response of your class.

We recommend strongly that you plan to use teaching aids, even if you merely jot down a word or two on a chalkboard from time to time to impress a point on the class. When you ask for a number of answers to a question, as in brainstorming, always jot down each answer in capsule form, to keep all ideas before the group. If no chalkboard is available, use a magic marker on large sheets of newsprint over a suitable easel. A printer can supply such paper for you at modest cost.

Once you have decided what visual or audio aids you will use, make sure *all* the necessary equipment is on hand *before* classtime. If you use electrical equipment such as projector or recorder, make sure you have an extension cord available if needed. For chalkboards, have chalk and eraser. That's obvious, of course, but small details are easily forgotten.

Encourage class members to bring Bibles or New Testaments to class and use them. It is good to have several modern-speech translations on hand for purposes of comparison.

Getting Started Right

Start on time. This is especially important for the first session for two reasons. First, it will set the pattern for the rest of the course. If you begin the first lesson late, members will have less reason for being on time at the others. Those who are punctual will be robbed of time, and those who are habitually late will come still later next time. Second, the first session should begin promptly because getting acquainted, explaining the procedure, and introducing the textbook will shorten your study time as it is.

Begin with prayer, asking the Holy Spirit to open hearts and minds, to give understanding, and to apply the truths that are studied. The Holy Spirit is the great Teacher. No teaching, however orthodox and carefully presented, can be truly Christian or spiritual without His control.

Involve everyone. The suggested plans for each session provide a maximum of participation for members of your class. This is important because—

1. People are usually more interested if they take part.
2. People remember more of what they discuss together than they

do of what they are told by a lecturer.

3. People like to help arrive at conclusions and applications. They are more likely to act on truth if they apply it to themselves than if it is applied to them by someone else.

To promote relaxed involvement, you may find it wise to—

1. Have the class sit in a circle or semicircle. Some who are not used to this idea may feel uncomfortable at first, but the arrangement makes class members feel more at home. It will also make discussion easier and more relaxed.

2. Remain seated while you teach (unless the class numbers over 25).

3. Be relaxed in your own attitude and manner. Remember that the class is not "yours," but the Lord's, so don't get tense!

4. Use some means to get the class better acquainted, unless all are well-known to each other. At the first meeting or two each member could wear a large-lettered name tag. Each one might also briefly tell something about himself, and perhaps tell what, specifically, he expects to get from this study.

Adapting the Course

This material is designed for quarterly use on a weekly basis, but it may be readily adapted to different uses. Those who wish to teach the course over a 12- or 13-week period may simply follow the lesson arrangement as it is given in this *Guide,* using or excluding review/examination sessions as desired.

For 10 sessions, the class may combine four of the shorter lessons into two. The same procedure should be followed for five sessions. However, if the material is to be covered in five sessions, each one should be two hours long with a 10-minute break near the middle. Divide the text chapters among the sessions as needed.

An Alternate Approach

The lesson plans outlined for each session in this *Guide* assume that class members are reading their texts before each class meets. The teacher should make every effort to spark interest in the text by giving members provocative assignments (as suggested under each session) and by such methods as reading aloud an especially fascinating passage (very brief) from the next week's text.

When for any reason, most of the class members will *not* have read the text in advance, (as when the class meets each evening in Vacation Bible School and members work during the day, or as in the first session, when texts may not have been available previously), a slightly different procedure must be followed.

At the beginning of the period, divide the class into small study groups of from four to six persons. Don't separate couples. It is not necessary for the same individuals to be grouped together each time the class meets— though if members prefer this, by all means allow them to meet together regularly.

As teacher of the class, lead one of the study groups yourself. Appoint a leader for each of the other groups. If people are reluctant to be leaders, explain that they need not teach and that they need no advance knowledge of the subject.

Allow the groups and their leaders as much as half an hour to study the textbook together. Then reassemble the class. Ask leaders to report findings or questions of unusual interest or that provoked disagreement. Ask the class the questions you want discussed, and allow questions from your students. Be sure to summarize in closing, what has been studied. Finally, urge each member of the class to make some specific application of the lesson to his life. Use any of the material in this *Guide* that is appropriate and for which you have time.

For additional help, see Kenneth Gangel's *24 Ways to Improve Your Teaching* (Victor, 1974).

Instructions for Victor Multiuse Transparency Masters

The removable center section in this guide provides Victor Multiuse Transparency Masters as important helps for your teaching of this course. They are numbered consecutively and show with what sessions they should be used. The guide gives specific directions for when and how to use each MTM in the lesson material.

To remove the MTMs, open up the two staples in the center of this book and pull out the MTMs. Close the staples again to keep the rest of your guide together. Straighten out the MTMs and file them flat in a regular file folder.

Making Transparencies

You may make your own transparencies inexpensively through the use of these transparency masters. This can be done in at least three ways:

1. Thermal copier (an infrared heat transfer process such as 3M's Thermofax is probably the fastest). Simply pass the MTM with the appropriate film on top of it through the copying machine (at the correct setting). The color portions printed on the MTM are designed not to reproduce.

2. Electrostatic process (such as Xerox). Take care to use the correct film for the right machine. Make sure the glass is clean. Some color on the MTM will come out gray. On certain MTMs some information, printed in a special light color, will NOT reproduce on machine-made transparencies. This gives you extra information to share orally or to write onto the transparency. This way you can control attention by adding material step-by-step. (You'll have all the "answers" on the original MTM.)

3. Trace your own MTM on a transparency film. With minimum artistic ability, you can place a sheet of film over the MTM and trace the major parts of the illustration. Exactness is not necessary and stick figures can be drawn over the printed figures. Block letters can be traced over the printing on the MTM. For best results, use clear 8½" x 11" sheets of polyester or mylar film (acetate works, but curls).

To write on the transparencies, use fiber-tip pens. You should have "erasable" or nonpermanent pens if you wish to reuse the film (these wash off with a damp cloth). Use permanent pens if you want to reuse the same visual aid. You may want to make the basic image with a permanent pen and add other material as needed with an erasable pen.

By tracing your own transparencies, you can make overlays. To do this, trace different parts of the *same* MTM onto *different* sheets of film. First, show only one part of the illustration on the bottom film. As the lesson progresses, lay other films on top of it to complete the MTM.

Don't give up if you don't have access to a copying machine. Try your public library, a school, or a printer. Or maybe there's a machine at your office, or at a friend's. Usually arrangements can be made, either by paying for the film or by bringing your own.

Other Uses of Transparency Masters

1. Spirit masters or mimeo stencils. From these masters or stencils you can run off material for each group member. Both of these can be made on a 3M Thermofax copier. From the master or stencil, as many copies as needed are then made on any spirit duplicator (such as a "ditto" machine) or mimeograph. The MTM may also be traced by hand or typed onto a spirit master or mimeograph stencil.

2. Visuals. For small groups, the MTMs may be used just as they are, as printed visual aids. It would be helpful to tape them to pieces of cardboard and then prop them up. Or you could put MTMs inside clear "report covers" and write on them.

3. Chalkboards. You may want to use the MTMs just as you do the other visual sketches in the guide. Copy the MTM illustration onto a chalkboard, flip chart, poster board, or sheet of newsprint, and use it as needed in your presentation.

Recommended Materials

1. Fiber-tip transparency pens for writing on film:
"Erasable" (removable with water from any film), such as Sanford's "Vis-a-Vis."
"Permanent" (removable with rubbing alcohol from acetate, mylar, or polyester), such as Sanford's "Sharpie" (Sanford Ink Co., 2740 Washington Blvd., Bellwood, IL 60104; 312/547-6650).

2. Clear or colored polyester (or mylar) film sheets for tracing or writing (Transilwrap Corp., 2615 N. Paulina, Chicago, IL 60614; 312/528-8000).

3. Thermal process film (also called infrared) for machines such as the 3M Thermofax. Transparency film in many colors, as well as spirit duplicator or mimeograph stencils, can all be "imaged" in four seconds on a Thermofax (3M Business Products, 303 Commerce Dr., Oak Brook, IL 60521; 312/920-4271).

4. Film for electrostatic copiers, such as Xerox (Arkwright-Interlaken Co., Main St., Fiskeville, RI 02823; 401/821-1000).

NOTE: These companies are manufacturing sources, but each can sell to you directly or refer you to dealers in your area. One convenient retail outlet for ALL of these items is Faith Venture Visuals, Inc., 510 East Main St., Lititz, PA 17543; 717/626-8503.

5. Two excellent resource books:
How to Make and Use Overhead Transparencies by Anna Sue Darkes (Moody, 1977).
Use Your Overhead by Lee Green (Victor, 1979).

Let's Just Praise the Lord!

Text, Chapter 1

SESSION GOALS
1. To get acquainted with one another and the course of study.
2. To find four praiseworthy aspects of God's person and work in Psalm 145.
3. To daily make the praise of God a high priority.

PREPARATION
1. Within each of us—however unpoetic we may seem—are psalms waiting to be expressed. Sound farfetched? Then take an excursion through the Book of Psalms. Though many of them were written by poetic David and musical Asaph, others were written by virtually unknown people—people like you and me, who longed to express their deepest feelings to God, and did. Though unknown to men, they were not unknown to God.

Warren Wiersbe suggests, "The psalms must be read with the heart as well as the head" (*Text,* Preface). As you prepare the psalms in this course, let them touch your heart, and let them teach you how to share your most intimate and honest expressions with God. Try keeping a journal of your experiences, ideas, and reflections. Why not encourage group members to do the same?

The first psalm in this course, Psalm 145, gets us started right: praising the Lord. As we praise the Lord, our attention is focused on Him and not on ourselves. By meditating on His qualities—goodness, righteousness, graciousness, compassion—we are convinced, "He will fulfill the desire of them that fear Him: He also will hear their cry, and will save them" (Ps. 145:19).

2. Scan the text, concentrating most on the Preface and chapter 1.
3. Note how MTM-1 compares the praising saint and the complaining saint. Prepare MTM-1 and Visual Sketch 1 (VS-1) for use during the session.
4. Be prepared to help group members get to know each other by providing name tags or 3 " x 5 " cards and stick pins. You will also need a supply of markers for this activity.

PRESENTATION
1. As group members arrive, distribute name tags on which they can print their first name and a catchy phrase about praise. Examples: Keep praising; Give yourself a faith lift—Praise the Lord; Praise changes things; Handle with praise.

Encourage those who already know others to introduce themselves to new members. Set the example by being genuinely friendly yourself.

2. Focus the group's attention on the personal aspect of the psalms as you begin by asking, **If you were to write a psalm of your life today, what would be the dominant theme? Fear, uncertainty, sorrow, happiness, weariness, hope, despair, love, hate? The gamut of human emotion is expressed in the psalms. Regardless of how the psalm begins, somewhere in the psalm the writer pours out his heart to God and finds he can then go on. What difference does praising the Lord make in our ability to cope with life?**

3. It is not necessary for group members to have read *Text,* chapter 1, prior to this session, in order to participate in a meaningful way.

Have the group read Psalm 145 responsively, unless too many versions are being used to make this type of reading feasible. In this case, be prepared to read Psalm 145 to the group.

What is the dominant theme of the psalm? Have group members give specific words from Psalm 145 to answer this question.

Display MTM-1 as you discuss, **Why is it that some Christians praise the Lord and others do not? In viewing the circumstances of life, how do the perspectives of the praising saint and the complaining saint differ?**

In Psalm 145, what is there about God that motivated the psalmist to express praise as he did? Find four praiseworthy aspects of God's person and work mentioned in this psalm. Put VS-1 on the chalkboard as the group lists the four aspects.

4. *The greatness of God.* **In what ways is God great? Besides the four ways God's greatness is described in Psalm 145:3-6, how is His greatness described in Isaiah 40:3-31?**

5. *The goodness of God.* "Greatness without goodness would make God a selfish tyrant; while goodness without greatness would make Him willing to help us but incapable of acting." (*Text,* chapter 1, under the subhead, "The Goodness of God.") **How has God expressed His goodness to man from Genesis 1 up to the present? What other qualities of God's character are directly linked with God's goodness? What should our response be to the goodness of God?** Besides being thankful, we should want to repent of our sins and forsake them; we should be better able to face life without fear.)

VS-1
Four praiseworthy aspects of God's person and work: His *greatness, goodness, government* (righteous rule), and *grace.*

6. *God's righteous rule in this world.* **Psalm 145:11-13 talks about God's kingdom. How is this kingdom described? Why is God's righteous rule in this kingdom important to us as Christians?**

7. Discuss the fourth aspect of God's person and work mentioned in Psalm 145—His *graciousness.* **How does God exhibit His grace to believers? To unbelievers? What can we learn about God's creation from this psalm?**

8. Use the remaining time of session 1 to talk about some of the more practical implications of Psalm 145. You may choose to conduct this segment of the session in small groups. If so, be sure to provide the following discussion questions in handout sheet form:

• One problem Christian families often face, is how to make family devotions meaningful to everyone. **How does Psalm 145:4 encourage us to be faithful in maintaining this fellowship with God as families? What have you found especially meaningful in your family devotions? What methods, ideas, concepts can you share that will help others in this area?**

• **In America, the percentage of unemployed has reached two-digit figures. How will believing Psalm 145:14-18 get believers through lean, difficult days? How has God helped you through financially hard times? How can we reconcile God's goodness with the fact that some believers are hungry and destitute? If we do not share our material wealth with those less prosperous, are we frustrating God's purposes? What can we learn about God and His care for us from a lack of physical supplies?**

• **What can we learn about prayer from Psalm 145? For believers, is there such a thing as unanswered prayer?** (Encourage group members to give the rationale for their responses.)

• **Why is verse 20 an incentive to be witnesses for the Lord?**

9. Close with conversational prayer (brief sentence prayers in which one person mentions a specific thing and another picks up where the first person left off). Limit the prayer time to expressions of praise. Suggest that people base their praise on the ideas of Psalm 145.

ASSIGNMENT

1. Continue meditating on Psalm 145. As you encounter difficult circumstances this week, turn the negatives into positives with praise. Enter your expressions of personal praise in a journal (*Preparation* 1).

2. Read chapter 2 of the text. If time permits, read Ezra 1—10 and Nehemiah 1—6 to get the historical setting of Psalm 115.

3. Use ideas from this session in your family devotions.

God Is not Dead!   /   *Text, Chapter 2*

SESSION GOALS
1. To note parallels between the settings of Psalm 115 and today.
2. To understand what God is really like, and respond to Him with worship, trust, reverential fear, and praise.

PREPARATION
1. Read Psalm 115, keeping in mind that it was probably written during the time when Israel was rebuilding the temple and walls of Jerusalem. To better understand this historical setting, read Ezra 1—10 and Nehemiah 1—6. Write down some of the problems the people faced and similar ones we face today.

The writer of Psalm 115 makes four declarations about God which encourage *our response:* God is alive—*glorify Him;* God helps us—*trust Him;* God blesses us—*fear Him;* God is worthy—*praise Him.* Read Warren Wiersbe's explanation of this psalm in chapter 2 of the text.

2. Prepare MTM-2 for use as an in-class worksheet (see Instructions for Victor Multiuse Transparency Masters). You will need one copy for each small group.

3. Contact two group members early in the week and ask them to be prepared to read Psalm 115 to the group. Verses 9-11 of this psalm are particularly antiphonal in nature. Ask them to read the psalm responsively (one person reading a verse, or section of a verse, with the second person reading the following verse or phrase).

4. Be prepared to have your group sing the hymn, "O God, Our Help in Ages Past."

PRESENTATION
1. **How many of you remember the "God is dead" movement which was prominent in the United States several years ago? What are some of the factors that brought about that movement? As believers, are we making significant progress in combating this spirit of unbelief in our nation today? If so, how are we? If not, why not?**

2. Have your two group members, contacted earlier in the week, read Psalm 115 at this time. (*Preparation 3*)

3. Summarize the background information the author relates in the opening paragraphs of chapter 2 of the text to set the stage for Psalm 115. Have the group scan Ezra 1—10 and Nehemiah 1—6 as you make the following two columns on the chalkboard:

National problems faced
in restoring Jerusalem

National problems faced
in our country today

Compile a list of short statements appropriate for each of these columns. At the end of this activity, go back and circle similar problems listed in both columns.

4. Divide into small groups of no more than five. Distribute a copy of MTM-2 to each small group. Have each group choose one person to guide the discussion and another person to record the group responses on the worksheet. Careful study of Psalm 115 will provide the necessary answers for the worksheet. However, chapter 2 of text will help clarify in certain instances. Allow 15-20 minutes for the groups to complete this study.

5. After the group has reassembled, briefly summarize Psalm 115. Give group members an opportunity to express what they have learned, or ask questions about things that may still be unclear.

6. Direct attention back to the list of national problems faced in our country today (*Presentation 3*). **Why should a believer's response to a problem be different from an unbeliever's facing the same situation? Drawing from Psalm 115, what help would a believer find who is facing the problem of unemployment, for instance?** (Point out several of the problems listed and ask the group to discuss them.) **How could a believer answer the taunt of an unbeliever, "Where is your God? Why doesn't He do something?" How can believers prove that their God is alive? That He helps us and deserves our trust? That He remains faithful to His promise to bless us? And that He is worthy of our praise, regardless of the circumstances?**

Ask members to share recent instances when they have found God alive and able to deal with their problems. **What advice do you have for others who might be in similar, yet unsolved, dilemmas?**

7. As your closing prayer, read or sing together Isaac Watts' hymn, "O God, Our Help in Ages Past."

(OPTION) If you are able to find a copy of Leslie Brandt's book, *Psalms/ Now* (Concordia), read "114 and 115" to the group in closing. The author takes the Old Testament psalms and translates them into the words, phrases, and look of today. You will find these psalm prayers a helpful way to gain new perspective on the old and familiar.

ASSIGNMENT
1. Think of something in Psalm 115 that was especially meaningful to you and write it in your journal of personal psalms.
2. Read chapter 3 of the text.
3. Memorize Psalm 115:1 as the symbol of the reality of God's answer to your need. Though your affairs may look gloomy today, launch out in faith believing God is working in your behalf. Be assured that the answer to your problem is coming, and that it will give glory to God.

When Good Things Happen to Bad People

Text, Chapter 3

SESSION GOALS

1. To admit our struggles with God as we try to understand what He is doing in our lives and in the world.

2. To see how Asaph, in Psalm 73, reconciled the problem of evil in the world with his faith in God.

3. To view life in terms of eternal rather than temporal values.

PREPARATION

1. Read Psalm 73 and note the five stages Asaph went through as he struggled to reconcile what he believed about God with what he saw of God's dealings with himself and the world around him. Think about your own experience. Are you struggling with what you believe about God as you face a web of unanswered questions surrounding your actual life's experience. Do you sometimes feel like a phony because you're smiling on the outside when on the inside you're filled with anger and doubt?

As the author points out, "Some of the greatest saints in the Bible had their struggles with God, trying to understand what He was doing in their lives and in the world." Remember Job and Jeremiah and Habakkuk and David in Psalm 37? Each of them struggled to understand why a good God would allow evil to prosper and the godly to suffer. Asaph spoke for them and every struggling saint when he admitted, "As for me, my feet were almost gone; my steps had well-nigh slipped" (Ps. 73:2).

In time, Asaph reached the "right" conclusion: "My flesh and my heart faileth: but God *is* the strength of my heart, and my portion forever" (Ps. 73:26).

2. Do you know of a group member who has seriously doubted God, yet ultimately reached a place of victory similar to that Asaph describes in Psalm 73:21-28? Early in the week, ask this person to be prepared to tell about his experience. It is important for the group to understand that God does not frown on us when we doubt Him. Rather, He desires that our doubts draw us into a closer relationship with Him.

3. Be prepared to have group members draw during this session. You will need a supply of paper, pencils, crayons or felt-tip pens. Members can put their artistic skills to work as they sketch caricatures of people who give a calm, smiling exterior when inwardly they feel frustrated because of unanswered questions and doubts concerning God and His ways. Have group members caption their sketches with clever quotes such as: • *Why be good? It's the bad who have it made.* • *The godless prosper while the godly suffer. Is it really worth it to be a believer?* • *What I believe about God just*

doesn't seem to fit with the things happening in my life. What good is my faith?

4. A number of good books have been written which address the problem of evil and suffering in the world in light of God's character. Check your church library or Christian bookstore for the following titles: *The Suffering God* (InterVarsity Press); *Where Are You God?* (Victor); *A Loving God and a Suffering World* (InterVarsity Press).

5. MTM-3 shows a believer at the crossroads of doubt. Psalm 73:16-28 shows why he took the right step.

PRESENTATION

1. In any group of believers, people are in various stages of Christian experience. But whether we are babies in Christ or mature, Spirit-filled believers, all of us at some time have struggled, or will struggle, with a faith in God that wavers because His ways seem to contradict what we believe about Him or His Word. Sometimes we are afraid to be really honest about our faith struggles. We try to disguise an angry heart by presenting a smiling face to our Christian friends and unbelievers.

Divide into small groups and give each group a sheet of paper and something with which to draw. Instruct them to draw caricatures like those described in *Preparation 3*. Give your groups about 7-10 minutes to complete their sketches before having them "show and tell" a little about them.

Direct the group to Psalm 73 and Old Testament believer Asaph's struggle. Asaph asked, *Why is there evil in the world? Why do bad things happen to good people and good things happen to bad people? Is it really worth it to be a believer?* Discuss Asaph's questions with your group. Encourage those who are struggling with doubt to freely express themselves.

2. Read Psalm 73 with the group and discuss the following questions:

• **On what basis did Asaph confirm his faith in God?** (v. 1)

• **If Asaph was not struggling with doubt because of sin in his life (v. 13), then why were his feet slipping, and why did he lack the enjoyment of God's goodness in his life?** (vv. 2-3)

• **What about the wicked upset Asaph? What about their lives caused him to question what he knew about God?** (vv. 3-12) Asaph was upset because of their prosperity (vv. 3-5), pride (vv. 6-9), and popularity (vv. 10-12).

•**When Asaph looked within, what immediate conclusion did he reach?** (vv. 13-15) He had made a big mistake by trusting God and keeping his life clean; he was not receiving any special blessing from God. While the wicked woke up in comfort, Asaph met the day with chastening.

Display MTM-3. Asaph stood at the crossroads. Behind him were all his past experiences of God's goodness and faithfulness. But now he was surrounded by the wicked's prosperity. What should he do? Pretend he was living victoriously? Go with the shallow, godless crowd? Would abandoning his faith in God bring him happiness? No. He knew the truth and could not turn his back on it.

• **Why didn't Asaph confide in another believer?** (v. 15) **Does this mean that honest sharing with one another displeases God?** Asaph didn't want to offend younger saints who had not yet faced some of these deeper problems. However, note that Asaph did not pretend all was well; he admitted he needed help and went to the One who could meet his deepest needs.

• **What right step did Asaph take?** (vv. 16-20) Asaph went to the temple and laid his case before God. It was there that he came to understand how the wicked would end, and that he was blessed to have been chosen by God.

• **What insight about himself did Asaph receive?** (vv. 21-22) He had been thinking and acting like an animal—concerned primarily with material and physical things. He had been walking by sight and not by faith—thinking like the people of the world who are concerned only for immediate gratification. Wrong thinking inevitably leads to wrong living. Asaph stopped just in time.

• **What did Asaph perceive about his future?** (vv. 23-28) God was his present source of joy and comfort; God would be his future. When he evaluated time in light of eternity and earth in light of heaven, he knew that because he had God, he had everything!

• **Did the situation around Asaph change?** No, but he changed. Read verse 28 together.

3. If you followed through with the suggestion in *Preparation 2,* ask for his or her input now.

4. **Based on Psalm 73, what principles for life can you think of?** List group members' suggestions on the chalkboard as they are volunteered. Some ideas to get you started are: *Walk by faith not by sight; God's Word is true no matter what our circumstances are; take the long view rather than the short sight of life; don't abandon the eternal for the temporal; God is the strength of our heart and portion forever.*

5. **How would you answer the unbeliever who asks, "Why should I become a believer? Why do I need God? What can God do for me that I can't do for myself? Aren't Christians the real losers of this world?"**

6. Close with conversational prayer.

ASSIGNMENT

1. Express your doubts to God by writing them in your journal of personal psalms.

2. Keep reaffirming your faith in God even though you may still be struggling with doubts. Faith will return.

3. Memorize Psalm 73:23-26 or another verse that speaks to your need.

4. Read chapter 4 of the text.

Happiness Is—? / *Text, Chapter 4*

SESSION GOALS
1. To state different definitions of happiness.
2. To examine three vivid biblical pictures of happiness.
3. To personally appropriate the happiness Jesus Christ offers.

PREPARATION
1. Read Psalm 126. Which event in your life caused you the greatest happiness? Why? What was the basis of the people's happiness in Psalm 126?
2. Scan chapter 4 of the text. Are you experiencing the *freedom, fullness,* and *fruitfulness* available to you in Christ?
3. Are you making the best use of your visuals? Can you improve your presentation of them? Note the suggested use of MTM-4 and VS-2 in the *Presentation.*

PRESENTATION
1. Ask members to state different definitions of happiness. Include your own. Warren Wiersbe defines happiness in the first few paragraphs of chapter 4 of the text. Here are a few more to whet the interest of your group: *"A good bank account, a good cook, and a good digestion."* (Jean-Jacques Rousseau) *"The strength and happiness of a man consists in finding out the way in which God is going, and going in that way too."* (Henry Ward Beecher) *"The only ones among you who will be really happy are those who will have sought and found how to serve."* (Albert Schweitzer)
How have your ideas of happiness changed in the past five years? Why have they changed? What, if any, irony do you see about happiness? (The "things" and "pleasures" intended to make us happy often leave us most unhappy.) **How would you describe a truly happy person?**
2. Happiness is an emotion that is more easily described than defined.
Display MTM-4 as the group reads Psalm 126 which describes happiness in three vivid pictures: *freedom, fullness, fruitfulness.* Each of us can experience the happiness described, no matter how blue or out of sorts we may feel now.
Have your group count off in threes. To find the historical setting of Psalm 126, assign each group one of the following three Scripture passages: (1) 2 Kings 18—19; (2) 2 Chronicles 32; (3) Isaiah 36—37. After several minutes of personal study, have the group reconstruct the historical setting by sharing what they have learned in reading these passages.
Note the contrasts of the people's emotions in Psalm 126:1-3. People who have been dominated by a foreign power and are then liberated can best understand the kind of joy these people experienced.
HAPPINESS IS FREEDOM. **How do some people's ideas of freedom to enjoy**

sin actually contradict the reality of happiness? What is the high price of enjoying the pleasures of sin? (Titus 3:3) Enslavement to various lusts and pleasures is the price tag.

• **What other kinds of bondage do people live in?** Fear, hopeless circumstances, other people's expectations, handicaps, hopeless future, etc.

• **In what ways does Jesus make us truly free?** Have group members look up the following Scriptures: Luke 4:18-19; John 8:32, 36; Rom. 7:1-6; 8:1; 1 Cor. 10:13; 15:50-58; Col. 1:13-14.

HAPPINESS IS FULLNESS. **How are dry, empty watercourses in the desert a good picture of our world today?**

• **Where can thirsty, unsaved people find true satisfaction?** See John 4:10ff; 7:37-39.

• **How do believers know they have adequate resources in Jesus?** See John 1:16; John 4:10-14; Col. 1:19; 2:9-10.

• **How can we experience the fullness of Christ every day?** Look up Acts 6:4; Eph. 5:18; Phil. 1:11; Col. 3:16; 1 Peter 1:8.

• **How would you answer a Christian who says, "I feel so dry and empty. How can I experience the happiness of fullness in Christ?**

HAPPINESS IS FRUITFULNESS. **What dilemma faced the delivered people in Psalm 126:5 and 6?**

• **What contrasts do we find between the first half of the psalm and the last?** The deliverance of the city was a sudden miraculous event, but the sending of a harvest is gradual and natural. God alone delivered the city, but He asked man's help to plow, sow, water, and reap a harvest. In the first part of the psalm, there was singing; in the last, weeping.

• **What do we learn from these contrasts?** Life is made up of a variety of experiences, and God works in our lives in a variety of ways. Sometimes He surprises us by sudden answers to prayers; other times we must wait for the answer, like a farmer patiently waiting for a harvest. Sometimes God works alone; other times He expects us to do our part. At times He works for us; other times, He works in and through us to accomplish His will.

• Discuss the statement: **"You can't outguess God."** What frequently happens when we try to put God in a box and anticipate how He will work?

• **How does the picture of sowing and reaping illustrate that we are**

VS-2
Scriptural principles of sowing and reaping.

delivered so that we can serve? Use VS-2 to illustrate two fundamental principles of life found in Galatians 6:7 and 2 Corinthians 9:6-8.

• Discuss: the seed we sow (Job 4:8; Prov. 6:16-19; 16:28; Gal. 6:7-9); the workers (John 4:31-38; 1 Cor. 3:6-9); the moods we sow in (Ps. 126:5-6; Acts 20:19, 31).

3. **In your own words, compare Satan's formula for happiness with Christ's** (see the last six paragraphs of chapter 4 of the text).

In Jesus Christ, happiness is *freedom, fullness,* **and** *fruitfulness.* **Is this the kind of happiness you are experiencing in your life today?**

4. Have group members pray together in pairs. Encourage them to pray conversationally using short sentences so that there is a spontaneity about it.

ASSIGNMENT

1. Evaluate the source of happiness in your life. Is it based on the freedom, fullness, and fruitfulness Jesus Christ offers? Record your thoughts in your journal of personal psalms.

2. Keep in mind the three pictures of happiness illustrated on MTM-4.

3. Read chapter 5 of the text.

Come Clean! / *Text, Chapter 5*

SESSION GOALS

1. To see how foolish it is to try and hide our sins from God.

2. To explore God's remedy for sin and recognize the guilt that unconfessed sin brings.

3. To confess our sins to God so that we can experience the joy of His cleansing.

PREPARATION

1. Psalm 32 is the honest expression of a man who has been hiding his sins for almost a year, but who finally surrenders his heart and will to God and finds joy once more in a restored relationship with Him.

Every saint can identify with the phases David went through as he tried to deal with his own sin. When ignoring it didn't work, he decided to endure God's chastening hand. But God's relentless love would not allow David to live estranged from Him. In desperation, David acknowledged his sin and found forgiveness and the joy of restoration.

Take a minute right now to confess any known sin so that the Holy Spirit is free to use you in guiding others to the same place of cleansing.

2. Print the following text quote on a flip chart or overhead transparency: "Apart from Jesus Christ, there is no solution to the problem of sin and guilt and the sad results of sin and guilt in the human life. The psychiatrist can alter the symptoms, but he cannot get to the root cause. Religion can temporarily encourage the emotions, but it can never cleanse the heart. Only Jesus Christ can deal finally and fully with the problem of sin in the life."

3. Early in the week contact a male group member and ask him to prepare a first-person narrative of David's sin recorded in 2 Samuel 11—12. This will set the stage for Psalm 32. As part of the account, have him read Psalm 32 using a recent translation or paraphrase. If he is willing, have him dress as King David.

4. Prepare MTM-5 and VS-3.

5. Type each of the four situations explained in *Presentation 5* on 4 " x 6 " cards.

PRESENTATION

1. **We have seen the contrasts in the lives of the good and the ungodly in each of the psalms studied to this point. What are some of the contrasts you remember?** Have the group briefly review Psalms 145, 115, 73, and 126 by recalling these contrasts.

Which verses or passages have been the greatest source of comfort or help to you? How have you grown in your appreciation of God's work in your heart and circumstances?

2. We have every means we need to live consistently in fellowship with the Lord, yet sometimes we still sin against Him. When this happens, our perception of His will becomes blurred and our fellowship sterile and meaningless.

Read the text quote mentioned in *Preparation 2*.

3. Introduce King David (*Preparation 3*) and have him set the historical context of Psalm 32 by giving his first-person narrative of the situation. End the presentation with the reading of Psalm 32.

4. Use the following series of questions to help the group more clearly understand Psalm 32:

• **This one event was an ugly blemish on David's life, but in the overall assessment, how did God see his life?** (See 1 Kings 15:3-5.)

• **What four stages did David work through as God dealt with the sin in his life?** (Use MTM-5 as you discuss these stages.)

STAGE 1—David finally faces his sin (Ps. 32:1-4).

STAGE 2—David contritely confesses his sin (v. 5).

STAGE 3—David joyfully receives God's forgiveness (vv. 6-7).

STAGE 4—David confidently faces life again (vv. 8-11).

• **What three different words did David use in Psalm 32 to describe what he had done?** *Transgression* (v. 1) which means "rebellion"; *iniquity* (v. 2) is "to be twisted or crooked"; *sin* (v. 5) is "to miss the mark."

• **Why does God chasten His children?** Hebrews 12:1-13 affirms that chastening is God's loving way of bringing His rebellious children to repentance.

- **If we know we are living in sin and God doesn't chasten us, what does that tell us about ourselves?**
- **Why does covering up sin invite emotional and psychological problems?** (Prov. 28:13; 1 John 1:5-10)
- **What is the difference between genuine confession of sin and merely saying, "I'm sorry"?** Have a group member look up and read Psalm 51:3-4, 16-17. Apply this Scripture to VS-3 as you discuss what true confession involves.

Ask yourself this question: "**Am I truly confessing my sin or am I really only excusing sin and looking for a way to escape the consequences?**"

- **How is a righteous God able to forgive guilty sinners?** Summarize what Warren Wiersbe says about God's grace in light of Romans 4. Review the meaning of the words: *forgiven; covered; imputed.*
- **What two things in David's life were evidence of his sin and broken fellowship with God?** (Loss of joy; lack of confidence.)
- **When David finally confessed his sin and moved back into the light of God's blessing, of what was he confident?** God's guidance (vv. 8-9); grace (v. 10); gladness (v. 11).
- **How does disobedience erode our confidence in God and ultimately in ourselves?**

5. Divide into four small groups. Give each group a card with one of the following four situations (*Preparation 5*):

(GROUP 1) Since childhood, Kevin has been programmed by his parents to say, "I'm sorry," every time he does wrong. Now that Kevin is an adult, he uses the words like a magic formula to get him out of painful predicaments. Recently his wife Sandy refused to accept his apology. "You're not really sorry," she sobbed. "You just think you can get away with anything if you say those words." Angry and hurt, Kevin and his equally troubled wife shared their disagreement with a spiritually mature friend. The friend said. . . .

Based on this discussion from Psalm 32, how could the friend help Kevin see his mistake?

(GROUP 2) Paul has been praying for guidance about an important decision. "God is silent," he complained to his pastor, "and I must know by

VS-3
True confession involves acknowledging and agreeing with God about our sin, but it also includes a broken heart and surrendered will.

True confession involves:	
acknowledging & agreeable lips	👄
a broken heart	💔
a surrendered will	🧑

Thursday whether or not to make this move." The pastor counseled. . . .

Based on Psalm 32, what could the pastor say to help Paul?

(GROUP 3) Audrey has had more than her share of troubles. Each new crisis threatens to destroy her emotionally. Though a believer, Audrey was named corespondent in a divorce case five years ago. Audrey has confessed her sin, but she feels nothing has gone right for her since. Her Bible study group has come to counsel and comfort her.

Based on Psalm 32, what hope can they offer her?

(GROUP 4) Kate has made a choice that could wreck her marriage, but she stubbornly insists she has a right to live her own life too. Though her pastor has counseled with her, she insists she is right. Her pastor feels there is something Kate is hiding, perhaps even from herself, that is clouding her relationship with the Lord. The pastor answered his phone recently to hear a distraught Kate declare she is even ready to stop claiming to be a Christian.

How can the pastor reach her, if he follows the principles of Psalm 32?

Reassemble the group. Have each of the groups briefly describe its situation and suggest ways in which Psalm 32 can help in the situation.

6. Close with prayers of praise and thanksgiving after you read Psalm 32:11.

ASSIGNMENT

1. Is there something you need to confess to God so that you can experience the joy of His cleansing? Write a prayer of confession in your psalms journal.

2. Read chapter 6 of the text.

GOD'S SINGING SOLDIER

How is God speaking to unheeding man today? • What is the result of God not interfering with man's decisions? (Rom. 1:18-32) • How will God speak one day so man will listen? (Matt. 24:21)

Voice Three   THE DECLARING VOICE OF THE SON   (VV. 7-9)

We rejoice when we read that Jesus is the Son of God and reigning King. What other title does He have from which we tend to withdraw? • How will He exercise this capacity on earth?

Voice Four   THE DECISIVE VOICE OF THE SPIRIT   (VV. 10-12)

Through the Holy Spirit, God appeals to man to stop rebelling against Him. To what does He appeal? (3 things) • Discuss the statement: "One of our greatest problems today is the fact that man has a great deal of knowledge but very little wisdom." What is wisdom? • What does man become when he has knowledge but not wisdom? • How has humanism affected our world? • If the statement, "Everyone is serving something" is true, then what are some people serving today if they're not serving God? (Rom. 6:12-13; Titus 3:3) • What causes rebellion? • What does God think of pride? (Ps. 138:6; Prov. 6:16-17; Prov. 21:4; James 4:6) • What is the significance of the phrase, "kiss the Son" in Psalm 2:12?

"Do You Hear What I'm Saying?"

(Bible Study Worksheet for Psalm 2)

One of the most serious problems of modern life is noise pollution. We are surrounded by noise that we don't even hear because we are so accustomed to it! Added to the increase in noise is the increase in the number of voices that cry for our attention. How can we make sense of all the noise in our world today? Psalm 2 invites us to hear four voices and understand what they are saying (*Text*, Chapter 9).

Answer the questions below to find the solution to this problem.

Voice One THE DEFIANT VOICE OF THE NATIONS (VV. 1-3)

Against what are the nations rebelling? • Why do men rebel against God? • How does man's united rebellion reveal itself today? • What is the relationship between freedom and authority? (Find the equation for true freedom mentioned in the text.) • What evidences today show that lack of enforced authority results in chaos? • Why has man's attempt to break free from God's moral law only brought him into more bondage? • How does Psalm 40:8 define real freedom? Do you agree with the definition?

PSALM 115
Bible Study Worksheet

Study Psalm 115 using the questions below to understand what God is really like and how we can respond to Him in the right way. Use the *Text* if additional information is needed to answer the questions.

(1) The psalmist begins by repeating the phrase, "not unto us." What does this phrase seem to indicate is the writer's primary concern? (vv. 1-2)

(2) Why was Jehovah's "reputation" important to the nation of Israel? (See Isaiah 46:3-13.)

(3) Instead of giving in to the sarcastic taunts of the enemy, the writer ridicules their heathen gods. Make a list of the contrasts between man's self-made gods and Jehovah God (vv. 3-7). See also Psalm 135:13-18 and

GOD <u>IS</u> GOOD.

PRETEND
  ALL IS WELL?

MTM-4 Use with Session 4 of *Meet Yourself in the Psalms*

"If we are truly thirsting after
and deliverance, then... life wi
we see only ourselves; it will
we see God."

OUR PRAISE
TO THEE!

FE

OLD

MTM-8 Use with Session 8 of *Meet Yourself in the Psalms*

?

2. We must yield
   ourselves to Christ.

LD

3. We must depend
   on the Spirit of God.

5. We must
   trust God
   the everyday
   needs and
   problems of life.

IN GOD WE TRUST

ly.

How do we "reign" in lif

1. We must belong to Jesus Christ.

4. We must live for God's glory alone.

Two Aspects of Christ's M

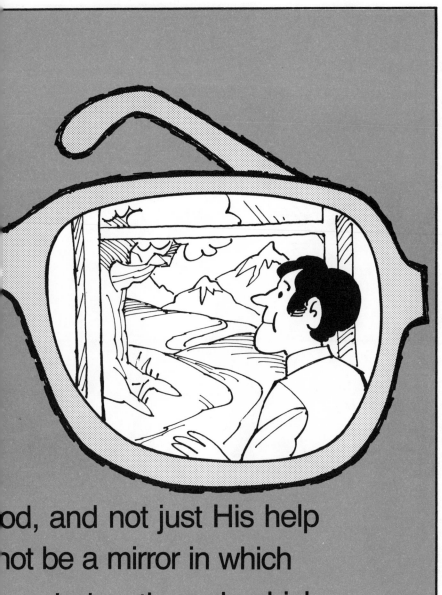

od, and not just His help

ot be a mirror in which

a window through which

FULLNESS

FRUITFULNESS

GO
WITH THE
CROWD?

?

(4) What irony does the psalmist see in those worshiping heathen gods and the gods themselves?

(5) Today, what kinds of false gods do men worship?

(6)?What three groups does the psalmist exhort to trust in the living God?

(7) What will those who trust in God discover about Him?

(8) The LORD promises blessing to those who trust in Him. What specific blessing was Israel seeking from Jehovah? Why was this blessing important to them as a nation?

(9) In what ways does God bless us today? Why does He *want* to bless us?

(10) What can we learn from verses 17-18 about praising God?

MTM-1 Use with Session 1 of *Meet Yourself in the Psalms*
©1983 by SP Publications, Inc. Permission granted to purchaser to reproduce this visual for class purp

Uplook for the Downcast / *Text, Chapter 6*

SESSION GOALS

1. To agree that Christians too can struggle with emotional depression.

2. To remember that as Christians we have divine resources available to help us work through depression.

3. To find out how Psalms 42 and 43 can help us overcome discouragement and depression.

4. To heed the advice of Psalm 43:5 and "hope in God" when we're tempted to focus on ourselves or our adverse circumstances.

PREPARATION

1. Read Psalms 42 and 43. Which speaks most clearly to your heart—the plight of the psalmist or the attributes of his God? Do you find yourself echoing the psalmist's questions? If so, follow through with him to his conclusion: "Hope in God; for I shall yet praise Him, who is the health of my countenance, and my God" (43:5).

2. Though the author is talking about the usual kind of discouragement, not the chronic kind of depression that requires professional care, you will find it helpful to ask a practicing Christian psychiatrist or counselor who has had experience helping depressed people to talk to the group about the symptoms of depression, its causes, and helpful treatment.

3. (READING RESOURCES) Check your church library or a local Christian bookstore for any of the following books which address the problem of depression: *The Masks of Melancholy* and *When Someone Asks for Help* (InterVarsity Press); *Overcoming Depression* (Westminster Press); *Beat the Blues* (Tyndale).

4. Answer each of the questions in the *Presentation* section so that you have worked through the problems prior to meeting with your group.

5. Note how MTM-6 and VS-4 contribute to the development of this session. Be prepared to use these visuals.

PRESENTATION

1. Divide into groups of three to six persons. Ask each group to make a list of 8 to 10 common causes of depression in our society. As each group reports, compile a list of causes on the chalkboard. **Which, if any, of these causes are exclusive to unbelievers?** Believers are not exempt from the problems that plague the rest of society.

2. If you were able to arrange for a Christian psychiatrist or counselor to speak to the group, introduce him at this time. Allow 10 to 15 minutes speaking and question-and-answer time.

3. **In what ways does an unbeliever deal differently with depression than a Christian? What drawback is there in trying to "escape" depression?**

4. Read Psalms 42 and 43 either responsively or verse by verse moving around the group.

After reading these psalms, what impression do you get about the author's view of life?

Do you agree with the author when he says, "Certainly there are various causes for depression, some of them physical; but basically, depression is selfish"? Why or why don't you agree?

In Psalm 42:3-5, what three causes of depression are expressed? His feelings had not been relieved (v. 3); his plans had not been fulfilled (v. 4); his questions had not been answered (v. 5).

Do you ever get discouraged when you have to change your plans? Do you ever pout because you feel sorry for yourself? Give group members an opportunity to share instances when they have felt the same way the psalmist did.

Why can't a change in circumstances alone cure depression? Look at the psalmist's experience in 42:1-2, 6-7. What did the psalmist see when he looked at nature? What did the Lord see when He looked at nature? (Matt. 6:24-34; 10:28-31) **How do we know that God is in control of the universe?** (Ps. 42:8) **How have times of getting back to nature helped you overcome depression?**

Warren Wiersbe says, "The most important thing about any difficult experience of life is not *that* we get out of it, but *what* we get out of it."

Changing our outlook on life is one way to get victory over discouragement and depression. Use MTM-6 to summarize this idea.

5. **Why is it depressing to continually look over our shoulder at the past, especially if we only see ourselves rather than God? What should we remember about the past?** (Deut. 5:15; 15:15; 16:12; 24:18, 22)

What *four* hopes does the psalmist focus on in Psalm 43:1-4?

What certain-to-be-fulfilled hopes can we as Christians rest on? (See Col. 1:27; 1 Tim. 1:1; Titus 2:13; 1 Peter 1:3; 3:15.)

6. To overcome depression, we must stop searching for reasons and start resting on promises. **Find 13 questions the author asked in Psalms 42 and 43. Note the 10 times he asked "Why?"**

Do you agree: "It is not wrong to ask questions of God, but it is wrong to

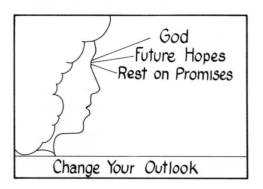

VS-4
Three changes that must take place in our outlook in life if we are to get victory over depression.

God
Future Hopes
Rest on Promises

Change Your Outlook

question God." Defend your response.

Even if God had answered all the psalmist's questions, would that have solved any problems and made him feel better?

From Psalms 42 and 43, find *six* promises the psalmist rested on.

Sketch VS-4 on the chalkboard as you recap three changes that must take place in our outlook on life if we are to get victory over depression.

7. Close with sentence prayers thanking God for the promises He's made to us, and asking Him to help us rest on His promises rather than search for the reasons.

ASSIGNMENT

1. In your journal of psalms, make a list of hopes and promises that you have found especially helpful. How will claiming these promises for yourself lift your depression?

2. Share with another hurting, depressed Christian the principles you ferreted out of Psalms 42 and 43.

3. Read chapter 7 of the text.

The Forgotten "I AM" / *Text, Chapter 7*

SESSION GOALS

1. To discuss two aspects of Christ's ministry found in Psalm 22: His suffering on the cross and the glory of His resurrection.

2. To respond personally, in faith, to Christ's death and resurrection.

PREPARATION

1. Psalm 22 is one of the great messianic psalms. Writing prophetically in this psalm, David speaks of how Christ will suffer death on a cross but also of the glory of His resurrection.

Before studying Psalm 22 in detail, read one of the four Gospel accounts of Christ's death and resurrection (Matt. 27:11—28:20; Mark 15:1—16:20; Luke 23:1—24:35; John 18:28—20:18) to remind you of the fulfilled "reality" of this prophetic psalm.

Try to imagine the Lord's suffering as He was forsaken by His Father, despised by the very people He gave His life to save, and humiliated as He died an excruciating death by crucifixion. Then turn your thoughts from His pain to the triumph of His resurrection. What love, thanksgiving, and praise we should feel for our Saviour.

2. Read chapter 7 of the text, noting the author's division of the psalm and his explanation of each verse.

3. Be prepared to use MTM-7 to help you visualize the two aspects of Christ's ministry spelled out in Psalm 22.

4. Have words and music available for "Alas! And Did My Saviour Bleed" and "Jesus Shall Reign." Both of these hymns, written by Isaac Watts, will help your group focus on the two aspects of Christ's ministry being discussed in this session.

5. Have paper and pencils available for use in *Presentation 2.*

6. Psalm 22 naturally leads to the plan of salvation. Pray that God will prepare the hearts of group members who may need to respond in personal faith to Jesus Christ. Review a *plan* which will enable you to simply present salvation to any who respond as the Holy Spirit prompts.

7. (OPTIONAL) If you were able to find a copy of Leslie F. Brandt's book, *Psalms/Now* (Concordia), be prepared to read Psalm 22 using this contemporary setting.

PRESENTATION

1. Begin by singing together all four stanzas of "Alas! And Did My Saviour Bleed." Then reiterate the incident Warren Wiersbe shares regarding the phrase "for such a worm as I."

In these days of self-awareness, we don't like to see ourselves as "worms." We'd rather think of ourselves in more worthwhile terms. Isn't it good to know that *God sees us* as worthwhile? He confirmed this estimation of us when He sent His only Son to die for our sins. Now we can enter into a right relationship with Him. What a contrast to the Saviour's estimation of Himself and the crushing humiliation He endured when He died to pay the penalty for our sins.

2. Explain how Psalms 22, 23, and 24 are a trilogy describing the "shepherd" ministries of Jesus Christ. Psalm 22 speaks of the Good Shepherd who died for the sheep.

Divide your group in half. Appoint a leader for each. Distribute paper and pencils to each group.

Ask one group to *find three different kinds of suffering that Christ endured at Calvary based on Psalm 22:1-21.* Encourage this group to refer to the Gospel accounts of Christ's death (*Preparation 1*) to grasp more fully how Christ suffered.

Have the second group *study Psalm 22:22-31 and explore the glory of the resurrected King.* Ask them to *note the three categories of people who share in this resurrection praise.*

After 15-20 minutes, have each group give a report on what they have learned.

3. **We have noted that Psalm 22 discusses two aspects of our Lord's ministry: His rejection and His glorification.** Display MTM-7 as you lead the following discussion:

• Several categories of people are mentioned in this psalm. Each contributes to the picture of Christ's rejection followed by His glorification.

Have the group pick out characteristics from Psalm 22 to fit the following captions: GOD • SAVIOUR • MOCKERS • BULLS & DOGS • SEED OF JACOB • BRETHREN • ENDS OF THE EARTH.

• **What false logic is expressed in verse 8?** A person who lives by faith will always be delivered from trouble. There is no contradiction or conflict between God's love and human suffering in the will of God. Jesus Christ was doing the Father's will, and the Father loved Him yet allowed Him to suffer. He was not delivered *from* suffering, but He was delivered *through* suffering, and He transformed that suffering into glory. **What implications does this have for our lives today?**

• **Why do you think the Gospel records of the Crucifixion do not emphasize the physical suffering of Christ on the cross?** Crucifixion with its degrading agony was a common form of execution when the Gospels were written. The important thing about our Lord's death was His spiritual agony of being made sin for us and being separated from the Father.

• **What comfort does verse 24 offer to suffering believers who seem to be crying out to a deaf God?**

• **Who will share in the anthem of praise which the triumphant Saviour now offers?** (vv. 25-31)

4. **What special message does Psalm 22 have for us as believers? For those who do not know Christ as Saviour?**

5. Because this psalm reveals the emotions and thoughts of Christ on the cross, we feel that it should almost be approached on bended knees. Worship a triumphant Saviour by singing together as you close, "Jesus Shall Reign."

6. (OPTIONAL) Read "Psalm 22" from *Psalms/Now* to summarize your thoughts for this session.

7. Ask group members to quietly meditate on Christ's suffering and glory. Direct their thoughts as you simply explain how they can personally know Christ as Saviour. In the silent moment following, let the Holy Spirit speak to individual hearts. Close with a short benediction.

ASSIGNMENT

1. What does Psalm 22 mean to you personally? Record a psalm of response in your journal. How will your understanding of the Lord's suffering and glory affect the way you live in the coming week?

2. Read chapter 8 of the text.

The Song of the Mid-Life Crisis / *Text, Chapter 8*

SESSION GOALS

1. To recognize that the foundation for a happy, godly old age is laid in youth.

2. To prepare now to meet the challenges of old age by building on three assurances about God found in Psalm 71.

3. To help or encourage a person of old age at the next opportunity.

PREPARATION

1. Regardless of how old or young you are, you will find the three assurances about God in Psalm 71 just what you need to face successfully the challenges of daily living: *God will protect you* (vv. 1-8); *God will be with you* (vv. 9-15); *God will use you to encourage others* (vv. 16-24).

Consider the age range of your group as you prepare to lead this session. Are most under 40? Then, focus on how to prepare right now for eventual old age, or how to help senior citizens presently facing the challenges of old age. If a majority of your group is middle-aged or older, focus on how they can make these the best years of their lives by concentrating on the assurances God gives about Himself in Psalm 71.

2. If possible, invite outside resource people to speak in this session. They can help make this an especially practical time of learning. Do you know of someone in the community who is successfully ministering to senior citizens in various capacities? A senior citizen who is coping with retirement exceptionally well? A Christian psychologist who could speak about the pressures and joys of old age? A banker or business person who could give constructive ways to financially prepare for retirement years? Invite one or more to speak to your group.

3. Though the youth craze has diminished as the median age of Americans has increased, people still need to be reminded that life doesn't stop at 30 nor begin at 40. Every year has its charm when lived in the will of God.

Use magazines such as *Modern Maturity* or relevant newspaper clippings or other data to portray the challenges and problems of the aged. By displaying these in your meeting room, you can help create an atmosphere for the subject of this session.

4. Read chapter 8 of the text and prepare VS-5 and MTM-8.

PRESENTATION

1. To make sure that your group's thinking is clearly defined, ask the group to determine what they consider to be the age range of "middle age" and "old age." Brainstorm good and bad things about middle age. List

these on the chalkboard.

Read Psalm 71 before discussing what the psalmist was feeling as he contemplated old age.

2. Point out the use of the phrase "all the day" (vv. 8, 15, 24). Put VS-5 on the chalkboard and comment: **One thing we all, young or old, have to do is learn to live a day at a time, depending on Christ** *all* **the day. If we try to carry the mistakes of yesterday and the worries about tomorrow, we will only turn today into defeat.**

3. Use MTM-8 as you discuss some fears that haunt people when they think of growing older: poverty, loneliness, illness, helplessness. **Look at Psalm 71:1-8 and decide what haunted the psalmist. What assurance about God encouraged him?** Look at the words trust, deliver, escape, incline, save, habitation, rock, fortress, hope, holden up, refuge, praise, honor. **What do you think was in the psalmist's mind when he prayed, "Be Thou my strong habitation, whereunto I may continually resort"? Why is it sometimes easier as one grows older to evade issues and escape from life?**

4. Warren Wiersbe points out that the assurance of God's protection is not something that we automatically know and believe. **When did the psalmist get his start in learning to trust God?** Quote the author: "We do not lay the foundations of our faith in our later years; we must lay them in childhood and youth. For some professing Christians, their 'golden years' are really 'leaden years' because they wasted their youth and did not lay solid foundations of faith." Discuss how we can help children lay solid foundations of faith, so that their golden years won't be leaden years. **What advice can be given to those who did not come to know the Lord until they were older?**

5. Read verses 9-15 of Psalm 71. **Why do so many older people feel like castoffs? What are some special temptations to guard against when we feel lonely and left out? What assurance about God did the psalmist use to cheer himself?** (vv. 14-15)

6. The first two assurances about God tell us how *God meets our needs and deals with our feelings.* The third assurance about God *frees us to reach out to others.* **What are some ways older saints can reach out to others?** (vv. 16, 18) Bring out the author's insights under the caption "God will use us to

VS-5
We need to drop yesterday's mistakes and tomorrow's worries and live one day at a time.

encourage others," chapter 8 of the text.

7. If any of the resource people mentioned in *Preparation 2* have come to this session, give them time to present their information and ideas.

8. Divide into small groups and let members build on insights gained from the resource people and this session as they discuss: **How can we help senior citizens we know, live fulfilled, God-glorifying lives? What practical help can we give them, as a group or individually, as we see them struggling with one or more fears?** (Aim for *practical* suggestions.)

9. **Note that the psalmist ends on a high note of praise and song. Compare verse 1 with verses 23 and 24. What lessons or principles can we draw from this psalm that will make us courageous victors no matter what our age?** If we fill our days with the Lord, He will take care of our enemies. Praise will defeat our foes. We must pray and rely on Him for help. Tell those around us of the great things God has done; they too will then praise our God.

10. Remain in small groups for prayer. Encourage the groups to focus on senior citizens they know of who have special needs. Also, thank God for the three assurances found in Psalm 71.

ASSIGNMENT
1. Read chapter 9 of the text.

2. Follow through with suggestions made in your small groups on ways of reaching out to others in need.

3. Write down three things you can do for yourself to prepare for your "golden years," or for someone you know who is already at that point (perhaps a family member).

SESSION **9**

Listen! God Is Laughing! / Text, Chapter 9

SESSION GOALS
1. To be aware of voices in the world today that are begging for our attention and obedience.

2. To discover the four "voices" of Psalm 2 and understand what they are saying.

3. To stop rebelling by responding to the Holy Spirit as He appeals to our minds, wills, and hearts.

PREPARATION
1. Read Psalm 2 from a number of different translations. "Listen" for: the *defiant* voice of the nations (vv. 1-3); the *derisive* (scoffing) voice of the

Father (vv. 4-6); the *declaring* voice of the Son (vv. 7-9); and the *decisive* voice of the Spirit (vv. 10-12).

2. Use chapter 9 of the text and MTM-9 to give you the outline of Psalm 2 and to help you prepare to lead this session.

3. Make a copy of MTM-9 for each member. You will also need to provide notebook-size paper and pencils.

4. Be prepared to use VS-6 as you discuss the equation for true freedom. VS-7 illustrates the results of man's decisions when left to himself without God.

5. Contact four group members early in the week and ask them to help you carry out the situation described in *Presentation 1*.

6. Before group members arrive, arrange the chairs in four circles.

7. (OPTIONAL) Compile a list of current book titles or magazine articles which deal with any of the "voices" that demand our attention today. For instance, *HIS* magazine (Inter-Varsity Christian Fellowship) addresses the issue of secular humanism in the March, 1983 issue. There are many other helpful voices that can be heard in the marketplace which can give us a balanced, Christian perspective. Look for them and share them resourcefully with your group.

PRESENTATION

1. As group members arrive, have them find a place in one of the four circles of chairs. Quietly direct each of the four persons you contacted earlier in the week (*Preparation 5*) to one of the four circles. (Do not have more than one per circle.) Secretly let the four "noisemakers" know that they should be distractingly vocal as the groups discuss an interest-baiting question such as: What are some of the national voices responsible for the pessimism prevalent in today's society? As the noisemakers become really loud, stop the discussions and say: **Loud voices get our attention, but they are not always the most worthy of hearing.** Let the rest of the group know that you prearranged for the four noisemakers to be an obvious distraction. Then talk about why the loudest voices in our society are not the ones we really need to hear nor are they the most trustworthy. God and His Son are speaking too, but we will not hear them unless we really want to.

VS-6
Freedom without authority is anarchy. Authority without freedom is slavery. True freedom is liberty under authority.

Freedom - Authority = Anarchy

Authority - Freedom = Slavery

$$\frac{Authority}{Liberty} = \begin{array}{l} TRUE \\ FREEDOM \end{array}$$

2. Give each group member a copy of the "Do you Hear What I'm Saying?" (MTM-9) worksheet along with extra paper and pencils. Each group should study the entire worksheet in order to understand the whole of Psalm 2. However, assign a different voice in Psalm 2 to each group, and ask them to be ready to give the vital message of the voice.

GROUP 1: The Defiant Voice of the Nations (vv. 1-3)
GROUP 2: The Derisive (*scoffing*) Voice of the Father (vv. 4-6)
GROUP 3: The Declaring Voice of the Son (vv. 7-9)
GROUP 4: The Decisive Voice of the Spirit (vv. 10-12)

Allow 20-25 minutes for this small group study. Participate in one of the groups yourself, but do not lead the discussion. Follow this time of study with group reports. Each group should highlight the vital message of their voice.

3. As the groups are reporting, draw attention to VS-6 as The Defiant Voice of the Nations is discussed. As GROUP 2 summarizes what they have learned about The Derisive (*scoffing*) Voice of the Father, use VS-7 to help group members see the devastating results of man's decisions when left to himself without God.

4. **Do you cringe before the pollution of our society and wallow in helplessness? Or do you have an open heart to hear God's voice in His Word so that you can move effectively as His witnesses in a polluted society? How can we be effective witnesses to the voice of the Father, Son, and Spirit in our world?**

5. If you were able to compile a list of current book titles and magazine articles which deal with the voices demanding our attention today, share it at this time. Give members a chance to tell of other written resources they know of which can help answer questions raised by these voices.

6. Close with prayer. Pray that we will be sensitive to the Spirit as He appeals to our minds, wills, and hearts.

ASSIGNMENT
1. Answer this question in your journal of psalms: Which of the four voices has spoken to you the loudest? Why has it?
2. Plan a witnessing strategy under the prompting and guidance of the

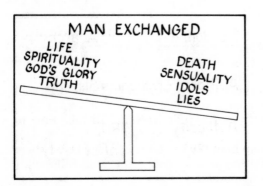

MAN EXCHANGED

LIFE
SPIRITUALITY
GOD'S GLORY
TRUTH

DEATH
SENSUALITY
IDOLS
LIES

VS-7
In Romans 1, it says that "God gave them (men) up." He let man have his own way. The result? Mankind exchanged truth for lies, God's glory for idols, spirituality for sensuality, and life for death.

Holy Spirit which will enable you to be a positive voice in the life of an un-saved friend.

3. Read chapter 10 of the text.

The Singing Soldier / *Text, Chapter 10*

SESSION GOALS

1. To discover from Psalm 27 how we can have victory over fear.

2. To recognize the importance of daily worship in our warfare against the Enemy.

3. To conquer fear by learning to *worship, walk,* and *wait* on God.

PREPARATION

1. Fear is an emotion each of us understands today. Whether our fear is triggered by inner anxiety or an outward enemy, it has the same paralyzing effect. In the psalms, David repeatedly expresses his fears. While David did have many enemies, he also learned how to handle his fears. His psalms often begin on a despondent note, but David always ends by praising God for giving him victory over his enemies. What was the secret of David's suc-cess in overcoming fear? How can this experience be ours today? Take a closer look at Psalm 27:4-5, and 8.

2. Read chapter 10 of the text noting who the singing soldier is and the warfare in which he is engaged.

3. Several definition-type quotes are mentioned at the beginning of chapter 10 in the text. Choose one of these quotes and write it on an overhead transparency, or be prepared to write it on the chalkboard as you start the session.

4. Contact a group member and ask him to write a "personal paraphrase" of Psalm 27. This psalm is easily adapted and can be effective-ly expressed in a personal and creative way. Using this kind of alternate ap-proach to normal methods of in-class Scripture reading is a good way to generate new interest in what is being read.

5. Look for magazine articles and newspaper clippings that deal with some of the causes and ways of coping with fear.

6. MTM-10 and VS-8 will help enrich your teaching, so take time to prepare them.

7. Some members in your group may need to know how to have a more effective personal Bible study. Be prepared to share methods of Bible study that you have found personally helpful.

PRESENTATION

1. Use your fear quote (*Preparation 3*) to get the session started. Have the group discuss fears that people have today. **What are some things you personally fear? How do you deal with your fears?** Be willing to share your own fears. None of us is completely fearless.

2. Introduce Psalm 27 by giving the situations David may have faced as he wrote it. It is thought that Psalm 27 was written during the time when King Saul was hounding David or when David's son Absalom rebelled against him. Whenever he wrote the psalm, he was facing real enemies (vv. 2, 6, 11-12) and he was tempted to be afraid (vv. 1, 3).

Have the group member you contacted earlier in the week, read his "personal paraphrase" of Psalm 27.

3. David was tempted to fear because of his enemies, but he did not give in to his fears. In this psalm, we can trace his experiences and discover how we can get victory over fear.

Divide into buzz groups and study Psalm 27:1-6 from the standpoint of a believer's *enemy, weapons,* and *secret power.*

4. Discuss the believer's warfare: **Why is a believer who somehow avoids persecution either hiding his light or compromising the truth?** (Matt. 10:32-39; 2 Tim. 3:12) **What light does 2 Timothy 2:1-3 shed on our position as soldiers of Jesus Christ? If we recognize that our flesh-and-blood enemies are really only tools of our real enemy, Satan, how will we deal with them?** (Matt. 5:43-48) **What weapons do we have to face our foes?** (Eph. 6:10-18) **Like David, our battles are won in private times of worship with the Lord. If we are losing most of the battles, what does that tell us about ourselves?**

5. **How would you answer a Christian who says, "Personal devotions are not a magic formula to ensure you a smooth path through life. I don't notice any difference in my life when I have my devotions from when I don't"?**

Study Psalm 27:4-6 to find out why David's time with the Lord made all the difference in his life. **What was David's first priority? In our worship today, what privilege do God's people have which David did not have?** (We can enter God's presence through the merits of Jesus Christ. David longed for this privilege, but could not have it. We have it, yet fail to take advantage of it.)

If time permits, discuss corporate worship. **What are some things that hinder worship in our churches today? If you could make your church services more worshipful, how would you do it? What do you think are some of the most important elements of corporate worship?**

What are some basic ingredients of true worship? (A prepared heart—genuine hunger to meet with God; recognition of the glory and power of God; praise with songs; acknowledgment of His power and might; trust.)

6. Use VS-8 to help you make the transition of atmosphere found in Psalm 27:7. David moved out of the place of worship into the marketplace and daily demands of life. Here is the true test of the genuineness of our relationship with God. **What can we learn about walking with God from verse 8?** Discuss the idea of "blessing breaks" mentioned by the author in the text. **Why is verse 11 a good one to memorize?**

7. A child convert in India prayed to her "Mother-Father" God when her Hindu family put pressure on her to give up her faith. **Where in the Word did she find a basis for such a prayer?** (Ps. 103:13; Isa. 49:15-16) **How does God deal with us as a wise, loving Father? As a tender, loving Mother? What experiences with the Lord have you had, that made you realize He does relate to you in these ways?**

8. The most difficult, yet important experience needed to help us overcome fear is *waiting*. For most people it is easier to war than to wait. **Share times when you found verses 13 and 14 to be true in your experience. What is involved in waiting on the Lord? What are some erroneous ideas we have about waiting? How should we use our time when we are waiting on God?**

9. Use MTM-10 to illustrate the characteristics of a singing soldier: *warring, worshiping, walking,* and *waiting*. Let this visual summarize and close the session. Leave your group thinking about this question: **Would you characterize yourself as a singing soldier?**

10. Ask for prayer requests. By now your group will most likely feel comfortable sharing genuine needs with each other. Use a small group format so that all who wish to may pray.

11. (OPTIONAL) Share or have group members share methods of Bible study that have proven effective in personal worship. Don't pass up this opportunity to practically meet the needs of some in your group.

ASSIGNMENT

1. Write down an instance in the coming week when you find God speaking to you in a time of fearing. Use your journal of personal psalms to record how you responded to the situation. Did you pause to worship Him and seek His face? If you did, did you find yourself encouraged in the Lord and better able to bless others through your life?

2. Commit yourself to daily spending time with God in worship. Make this a number-one priority even as David did.

3. Memorize Psalm 62:5-6 to help you the next time you find yourself in a fearful situation.

4. Read chapter 11 of the text.

5. Bring your journal of personal psalms to the next session.

VS-8
Are you one of God's singing soldiers who uses your secret weapons—prayer and praise?

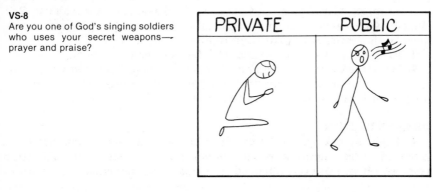

PRIVATE   PUBLIC

Life's Second Most Important Question

Text, Chapter 11

SESSION GOALS

1. To answer the question, "What is man?" from a secular and biblical viewpoint.

2. To understand our place in the universe by meeting three "kings" in Psalm 8.

3. To yield to Christ in faith and depend on His Spirit, so that we can live for His glory as we trust Him with the everyday needs and problems of life.

PREPARATION

1. Psalm 8 pointedly asks life's second most important question, "What is man?" Though man has always tried to answer the question from his own limited viewpoint, the writer David asks the question of the Authority on man, the Creator of man. Read verses 5-9 to find the answer David gleaned from his knowledge of God.

God crowned man with glory and honor! Then why isn't man acting like a king? Why is he in so much trouble when God gave him authority and dominion? There is something wrong, and Psalm 8 explains what it is through the eyes of three "kings."

2. Plan to involve group members in this session by assigning the following study projects to two members who are willing to spend time preparing. Be sure to contact these individuals early in the week. Group involvement is a good way to add depth and interest to your session.

STUDY PROJECT ONE: Find three viewpoints in Luke 15 which explain who man is. Be prepared to present both the biblical and secular views, drawing from the first three paragraphs of chapter 11 of the text.

STUDY PROJECT TWO: Explore what Romans 5—8 has to say about the power of the Spirit in the life of a yielded believer. Prepare a brief talk on the subject "Through Jesus Christ, we reign as kings." Chapters 4—7 of Wiersbe's *Be Right* (Victor) explains an often misunderstood and misapplied truth: Christians *are* to reign in life by Christ.

3. Be prepared to use VS-9 and MTM-11 during this session.

4. Write the question "Who am I?" in large, bold letters on several different colored sheets of construction paper. Post these in a number of prominent locations in your meeting room.

PRESENTATION

1. Begin by asking, "**Who am I? Who are you? What is man?**" This series of three questions is not intended to generate a verbal, group response. It *is*, however, intended to provoke thought. Use hand gestures

and a serious, provoking tone of voice to help communicate the real intensity of the questions.

Each of us wrestles with the question "Who am I?" until we find the answer that provides satisfaction and peace. Unfortunately, some people will not accept the Truth and thus go through life, groping for the right answer, but never finding fulfillment.

2. Have the resource person for STUDY PROJECT ONE present three viewpoints in Luke 15 which explain who man is. Provide an opportunity for others in the group to respond to and discuss their ideas and feelings.

3. **What man thinks of man may be important, but even more important is what God thinks of man.** Read Psalm 8 as a group.

God crowned man with glory and honor. But man isn't acting like a king. God gave him authority and dominion. Why, then, does he act more like a slave than a sovereign? The three kings of Psalm 8 explain what went wrong with man. Draw VS-9 one "king" at a time as each is discussed.

King Adam   Study Genesis 1:26-28; Psalm 8:5 and 100:3; Isaiah 43:7; Romans 5 to explain Genesis 3; and Romans 3:23 to find his lineage, his domain, his rule, and how he lost his throne and his crown.

Why must we know the story of our ancestor Adam if we really want to know who we are?

King Jesus Christ   From Adam we learned that God the Father *created* us to be kings. Now we will learn that God the Son *redeemed* us to be kings.

Study Hebrews 2:5-9; 1 Corinthians 15:47; Mark 1:13 and 11:1-7; Luke 5:1-11 and 22:34; John 21:1-6; Matthew 17:24-27; Romans 5; Hebrews 2:8-9; 1 Corinthians 15:27; Ephesians 1:22 and 2:4-6; 1 Corinthians 3:21-22; and Romans 6:14 to find His lineage, His dominion on earth, His purpose for coming, and how we reign as kings through Jesus Christ.

Ask for the STUDY PROJECT TWO report at this time.

From Adam, we learned that God the Father created us to *be* kings. God the Son redeemed us to be kings. How does knowing these truths help us find our identities?

King David   Study 1 Samuel 17 and Psalm 8 to see the parallels between the two passages. **Who is the enemy of Psalm 8:2? What did David**

VS-9
The three "kings" in Psalm 8 help us to understand man's place in the universe and how he is to fulfill it.

King Adam	Tells us who we are
King Jesus	Tells us how we can reign in life
King David	Tells us how to live like a king

know about the authority God had given man that gave him courage to stand up to Goliath's taunts? (Compare 1 Sam. 17:44-45 with Ps. 8:4-6.) How was David's position as anointed "king-in-waiting" similar to our experience as believers who have received the Holy Spirit? (1 John 2:27) We are not yet on our thrones, but we are seated with Christ on His throne. This gives us the authority to "reign in life."

How do we "reign in life"? Discuss five ways the author of the text answers this question by discussing MTM-11.

4. Respond to the statement: "The insignificant nuisances of life, if not handled properly, can keep us from conquering the big enemies that are sure to attack us!"

5. How can the message of Psalm 8 help a believer who has not quite found himself? Why does knowing we are created in God's image give us self-confidence and a sense of value to God? What message does this psalm have for an unsaved person who is trying to find himself through drugs, alcohol, personal ambition, etc.?

6. Give the group time to write a psalm in their journals expressing their feelings about being created in God's image, and being redeemed by His Son to reign in life through Jesus Christ. Some may volunteer to read aloud what they have written.

7. Form small prayer groups and echo David's beginning words of praise: "O Lord our Lord, how excellent is Thy name in all the earth!" Thank God for revealing to us the answer to life's second most important question. Pray for people you know who are still groping for this answer or who are hurting because they have misconceptions of their worth.

ASSIGNMENT

1. If you want praiseworthy thoughts to fill your mind when you feel worthless, memorize Psalm 8.

2. Read chapter 12 of the text.

3. Reread the psalms you have written in your journal. Do you feel that you are getting to know your Lord more intimately?

The Wonder of It All! / *Text, Chapter 12*

SESSION GOALS

1. To see the wonder of God's knowledge, presence, power, and judgment in Psalm 139 and how it relates to us personally.

2. To see how a condoning attitude toward sin leads to a weak view of God, which leads to a wrong view of His holy judgment.

3. To let the wonder of God lead us to worship, and help us put daily life into perspective.

PREPARATION

1. Read Psalm 139 and jot down what the psalm says about *you, God,* and *the wicked.* Also read chapter 12 of the text. Do you agree with the author that "Our modern-day loss of wonder has helped to make us shallow and hollow"? He further states that "Wonder and worship go together. Worship leads to depth. Wonder and worship help us put daily life into perspective, and perspective helps us determine true values."

This week, make it a point to spend some time each day worshiping the Lord, growing more and more in the wonder of His person through repeated reading of Psalm 139.

2. Be prepared to use VS-10 and MTM-12 during this session.

3. Have paper ready to hand out to group members for the activity mentioned in *Presentation 2.*

PRESENTATION

1. Draw VS-10 on the chalkboard. **When is God closest to us? During our mountaintop experiences? Or when some circumstance, disappointment, or tangled relationship plunges us into the depth of despair?** Our emotions play a part in our concept of God. Thus, we often feel that God is close to us in our triumphs and far from us in our defeats. Psalm 139 tells us about God's true relationship with His children.

2. Ask the group to spend five to ten minutes silently reading the psalm and jotting down in their journal of personal psalms what they now realize about themselves and God. (Distribute paper to those who did not bring their journals with them to this session.)

After this time spent in silent contemplation of themselves and God, ask them to share how they feel when they think of God. Surely one feeling is wonder.

Summarize the first five paragraphs of chapter 12.

3. Divide into groups of three to five. Have the small groups study Psalm 139 using the following caption as a guide: *Wonder of God—How does this aspect of God's character affect me?* Refer to chapter 12 of the text for further insight into God's relationship to His children.

4. Discuss the following questions with your group:

• **Why should we not study about God's omniscience in an abstract, philosophical way? When people do use this approach to God, what is usually the result in their relationship to God?**

• **Why do some believers read into God's omniscience a reason for fear, rather than comfort?** They think of God as being ready to clobber them if they get out of line, rather than the truth that because God knows everything about them, He brings them into the shelter of His providential care.

• **Why does God's omnipresence free us from worry?**

• **What dimension does believing in God's omnipotence add to our lives?**

• **What do verses 13-18 teach us about accepting ourselves? How do we know that God has a plan for our lives, and that we are fulfilled when we live our lives according to His plan?**

• **What does this psalm have to say about the issues of abortion, suicide, and "mercy killing"?**

5. Sometimes writers in the Book of Psalms express violent opposition to their enemies and ask God's terrible judgment upon them. Such Imprecatory Psalms—characterized by this call for judgment—seem inconsistent with the Christian revelation of forgiveness. **How do you explain this attitude?** The psalmist saw God's enemies as his enemies (compare 139:20 and 22). Look at the following biblical characters' attitudes toward sin and the sinner: Jeremiah (11:18ff; 15:15ff; 18:19ff), the Apostle Paul (Gal. 1:8-9), Jesus Christ (Matt. 21:40-44; 22:7; Luke 19:27). **How is modern society at odds with God's viewpoint of sin?** Their weak view of God gives them a wrong view of His holy judgment. **What do we as Christians need to guard against in our view of sin and sinners?** We must beware of taking a weak, inadequate view of sin or a sentimental one that is not the same as God's. **How does the revelation of the New Testament concerning punishment for sin shed light on the Old Testament viewpoint?** Note the author's explanation under the subhead, "The wonder of His judgment," paragraphs 7-11.

6. Let the group consider why Psalm 139:23-24 contains the prayer of a

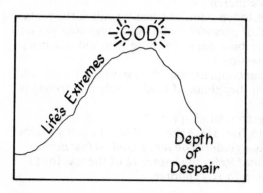

VS-10
When is God closest to us?

believer in harmony with his God. Display MTM-12 to give direction to their thoughts. **What connection is there between what we believe about God (His omniscience, omnipresence, omnipotence, and perfect judgment) and this prayer?**

7. Finally, have members work in pairs as they share from their journals some of the thoughts they jotted down in the first part of the session (*Presentation 2*). Have them tell which aspects of God's person evoke the most wonder in them. This sense of wonder will lead to praise and adoration which forms the basis of worship.

Close by having all repeat in unison Psalm 139:23-24.

ASSIGNMENT

1. Remember that "Wonder and worship help us put daily life into perspective, and perspective helps us determine true values." Try to take time each day this next week to read Psalm 139 so that you can grow in your sense of wonder and worship of God.

2. Think about what you have learned in your study of *Meet Yourself in the Psalms* and be ready to participate in next session's summation of the study.

Review

SESSION GOALS

1. To review the psalms and recall specific lessons that have changed our attitudes or behavior.

2. To commit ourselves to daily meet with God so that we get to know Him in a growing, intimate way.

3. To keep growing in the knowledge of who we are so that we will grow in our relationships with each other and with unbelievers.

PREPARATION

1. Skim through the text and review your notes. Decide which visuals you can use to make this a meaningful review session.

2. Reread your journal of personal psalms. What are some of the most significant lessons you have learned? Are you living out any commitments you made to the Lord? Have you learned to trust Him more? Are you able to respond to others confidently, knowing you are loved by God and created in His image? Can you see how His plans for you are being fulfilled and that your greatest potential is being reached?

3. Spend time praying for your members and for this final session together.

PRESENTATION

1. List the psalms covered in this study on the chalkboard with an identifying word or two about each.

2. Mention that **the past 12 weeks have given us an opportunity to get to know ourselves better as week by week we have been meeting ourselves in the Psalms.** Give group members a chance to share some of the thoughts they have recorded in their journals. Be prepared to share something yourself if you find members slow to respond.

3. Divide into four groups. Assign each group three psalms covered in the text. Have them scan the psalms and reiterate what they found there about *God, themselves,* and *the wicked.* Allow several minutes for this activity; then have each group give a summary.

How have these characteristics about God helped you in your relationship with Him? Are you better able to share yourself, your feelings, and your needs with Him? Have you come to better understand yourself? Are you able to relate to others in more loving, constructive ways? Are you more acutely aware of the price God the Father and His Son paid for sin?

4. Many of the Psalms are prayers. Close by finding sentence prayers in the psalms studied. These can be made into daily prayers. (See Psalm 27:7-12; 32:7; 42:1-2; 43:1-3; 115:1; 139:23-24; 145:1-2.) God welcomes all who "call upon Him in truth" (Ps. 145:18).